Follow That Sign!

Jhani's Personal Guide To Yard Sales

Jhani Monroe

Follow That Sign!
Jhani's Personal Guide to Yard Sales

For information regarding permission or additional copies, contact publisher:

KNOWLEDGE POWER BOOKS
25379 Wayne Mills Place, Suite, 131
Valencia, CA 91355
www.knowledgepowerbooks.com
661-513-0308

ISBN: 978-0-9854107-8-0
Library of Congress Control Number: 2012945579
Edited by: Dolly Ogawa-Amsk and Michelle Otis
Front and Back Cover Design: Clint D. Johnson
Interior Design: John Sibley, Rock Solid Graphic Arts

Printed in the United States of America

Table of Contents

Dedication

This book is dedicated to my husband Samuel because he didn't mind my leaving to go to yard sale after yard sale for so many years, Saturday after Saturday and even to this day. When he wasn't working on Saturdays, there was no question of the kids staying home with Dad. I think once he saw that I brought so many valuable treasures home, I believed he knew that I had a legitimate hobby. I bought a lot of practical things for everyone, even him.

My two older children got a lot of fun toys and many things to keep them busy. It's interesting that my husband only went out to a few sales with me over the years. I guess he was just seeing what it was really all about, but it just wasn't of personal interest to him. I appreciate him greatly for the support. I did like the few times that it would rain on a Saturday and that would automatically keep me in with my family. I've had many wonderful days Following That Sign with the arrow on it.

Of course, my father's selling influence is much remembered also. It helped give me my start and, unknowingly at the time, it would turn into such a fulfilling hobby and business.

Acknowledgements

First of all, I'm very thankful that passions stay with you, and when they are true passions you continue to pursue them through thick and thin.

I want to thank everyone that's ever given a yard sale, including myself. In most cases someone has pleased us with their merchandise and we have pleased someone else with ours. Outstanding!

Over the years I began to take notes about my interest in yard sales. I have recently found out that once you have so much experience and information, you have to do something with it. Every now and then I thought about a book, especially when someone went to yard sales with me and they saw how serious I was. A couple of people mentioned that I should write about it.

When you begin to do a task very well, confidence automatically sets in, and without realizing it you can become a professional. Some students study until they pass their subject, then they conquer the subject to become the teacher to teach what they know to students. I realize that practice can make perfect. In jobs that I have done in the past I liked repetition because my confidence would grow, and then I could be the best at it. Well, for me, going to and giving yard sales is something that I did over and over. I got better and better at it, at least that's how I feel about it. I just began to love it, a good healthy love for it! I think sometimes we take for granted things that we do over and over, not realizing that it could be one of our very gifts and purposes to share.

I didn't do anything about it for years other than keeping some of the notes. In 2009, my friend Sheryl Negash told me that I should really pursue writing a book. I paid attention to what she said, but I didn't know how it would happen. I want to thank her because she is definitely a motivator, a mentor, an educator, and someone special who really believes in success for all ages.

I want to thank the following people:

My son Jonathan who kept telling me to write a book about my marriage. Who knew that I would be writing any book? He must have had some insight regarding a book in general, so maybe someday a book about my marriage will surface;

My oldest daughter Samantha for being the first outside of my publisher to read the manuscript and give me the OK, in her opinion, to go ahead;

My youngest daughter Samara for being happy for me, but certainly going on with her own desires and making her usual noises as I tried to type;

Gospel artist Melanie Crisp for coming to my home and helping me work things out on the computer. The timing was perfect;

Glenda Banks who has a special place in my heart because she trusted me to do some things for her on the computer which helped inspire me to do the things that I needed to do to accomplish this great task in my life;

Marryan Marshall for going to yard sales with me many times and letting me drive her car because she felt that I knew what I was doing. She was such a blessing. She never even asked for gas money. That's just how she is;

My family who never ridiculed me. They were

interested in what I was doing and some of them periodically asked me to look for things for them. Special thanks to all family members who helped me in any way with my yard sales;

Friends who let me do yard sales for them, like Karen Davis who in turn told Wandra White and Denise Ammons. Karen's was the first yard sale that I ever did for someone else. She was getting married and I took her items to my Dad's house and sold them. I remember that she made $176. She had nice things and a lot of shoes. It was an interesting task at the time that gave me some joy, I was just working my hobby, and it brings back memories of how I just did it without even realizing that I was gaining such a passion;

Betty McFadden and Cherie Payne who spread the word about my business and referred people to me to assist with their yard sales – one being Sharon Walker whom I helped pack before she moved. She didn't have to have a yard sale because some items were sold by word of mouth and some were given away. She was so organized and knew exactly how she wanted everything done. I also gave similar assistance to her friend Minnie Grant not long after. She was so pleasant about everything;

My cover designer Clint Johnson who designed my first business card for my children's resale store more than 15 years ago. Now he's back with a one-of-a-kind cover for this book. I never thought that I would be upgrading something from the past that is really an extension of what my store was all about long ago, "mainly reselling." Thank you very much, Clint Johnson, for your great gift of design;

Pastors Fred and Linda Hodge who didn't hesitate to let

me work their yard sale. Also, Pastor Hodge spoke to me about yard sales being a business for me. I had never looked at it like that because I enjoy doing it so much.

Theresa Kirk and Pastor Linda Hodge again were forerunners for me in having their books published with Knowledge Power Books. Of course, I want to thank Mollie Williams with whom I spoke about my book. She so politely gave me her sister's business card, the #1 publisher Willa Robinson of Knowledge Power Books, who so gracefully accepted my manuscript. It is such a pleasure working with her.

To all who read this book, I hope you gain all the knowledge and power needed to have your yard sale or go to one but, if necessary, there is assistance always offered.

My Personal Story

This book is about my personal experiences of learning to have yard sales and how to go to them. I think my story offers everyone the knowledge of having a yard sale and shopping at them as well. As many yard sales as there are today, many people have never gone to one or ever given one, so the information is extremely helpful.

Besides telling my stories on how I started having yard sales and then going to them, another part of what I do is having yard sales for people, businesses, and organizations. Also, when someone is moving I help them pack, and if they want to have a yard sale they separate those items and have the sale before they move. This way they don't have to take the things they no longer want to their new dwelling place. It has been a great help to many people.

This is a hobby that I really love. It began with just curiosity then it turned almost into a career. Many times people's talent or creative skills have turned into their means of making a living, which is good. I have two degrees and I have worked in my profession, however, when the last charter school where I was teaching closed due to low enrollment, I was encouraged to work my hobby as a means of making ends meet.

Good Words about Jhani

"Jhani and I have gone to so many yard sales together and I have learned so much. She would tell me, 'Survey the area, and see if something catches your eye, so you don't miss out on something you really want.' Another one of her favorite sayings is, 'The early bird catches the worm.' Jhani always wanted to be first at the yard sales. She would tell me to always bargain. Ask, 'Is this price firm?' I still enjoy going out with Jhani but if she is not there, I feel confident to go alone because she has taught me so much."

Marryan Marshall
Lancaster, California

"Jhani Monroe has taken her love for the bargain and become the 'go to' expert for yard/garage sale success. My women's group experienced and benefitted from that expertise at our first annual parking lot yard sale where Jhani trained us in signage, led us in organization, showed us how to maximize sales, and infected us with her enthusiasm for the task. I encourage all sellers to 'follow Jhani's signs' for yard sale success."

Gwen Smith
Calvary Chapel Crenshaw, Los Angeles, California

How to Make Money Having a Yard Sale

The first yard sale that I knew about was my father's, and that was well over twenty years ago. I knew that he owned a store when I was quite young, so selling was just something he did. When he retired from his career, he started having yard sales at his house. His house was on a very busy street, so he didn't need to put yard sale signs up.

My father told me that one day he took his vacuum cleaner for repair. He watched the repairman fix it and said to himself, "It's so easy that I can do this." After that, he repaired his own vacuums and many others as well.

When he started having his yard sales, vacuum cleaners were his primary merchandise. They were well-repaired vacuum cleaners. He did very well for a retiree in his own front yard, and he even gave his customers a 30-day money back guarantee.

He talked about people having dirty vacuums. He could tell that they were clogged with dirt from all of the dust he had to clean out of them. Each time the vacuum cleaner I received as a wedding gift stopped working, he had no problem fixing it and telling me how dirty it was. He could clean things superbly; even a cast iron skillet would look like it had never been used.

He showed my brother and cousin how to fix vacuum cleaners as well. They became his young manpower and assisted him on Saturdays. Actually, Saturday was the only day he sold. My brother and cousin became excellent vacuum cleaner repairmen for the yard sales. My father also had other young assistants from time to time to help.

LIKE FATHER, LIKE SON, LIKE MOTHER, LIKE DAUGHTER, SOMETIMES

This is so interesting to me. My mother told me that my grandmother liked going to antique stores and she liked going to thrift stores. I like going to yard sales. This path seemed to have started long ago from the diverse experiences of shopping. Sometimes we might not realize that we have received some of our passions and talents right from the family tree.

IF YOU DON'T WANT TO SELL IT YOURSELF, LET SOMEONE ELSE SELL IT FOR YOU

Sometimes I would give my father the things that I didn't want anymore for his sales. Later, when I needed money, I would bring my things to his house to sell for myself or just get the money from him so he could sell them. I didn't always like to stay there and sell if I didn't have to. My father and I would sit on his front porch and chat about what things were worth. That was of great interest to me, just as the Antiques Road Show™ is.

One man's trash is truly another man's treasure. Many times people would drop off items at my father's to get rid of it instead of calling someone to pick it up. My dad was good at picking things up right off the streets and putting them in his pickup truck, restoring them like new, and selling them. I wish I had his old pickup truck, that's something I have yet to get.

DIAMONDS IN THE ROUGH

My Father knew what diamonds in the rough were all about; that's why he had no problem restoring things. He told me that some of the old pennies with the wheat on the back were worth keeping. I watched him collect coins, cans, newspapers, copper, odds and ends. Although he had an old coin collection, his last gift to us was a new gold coin.

ISN'T IT AWESOME HOW A CASUAL DAY CAN PRESENT LASTING INSPIRING PASSIONS?

What really inspired me to start having my own yard sales was my neighbor. She was also my sister's friend. One day she put her merchandise outside in the yard of the family units where we were living. I went outside and really took notice of her things. She had nice and expensive things. I couldn't afford many at the time, but I bought what I could. After seeing my neighbor work her sale, I was inspired to have my own.

TO HOLD ON TO, OR NOT TO HOLD ON TO, THAT IS THE QUESTION

First of all, I'm not one to hold on to everything that I have forever, so the idea of having a yard sale at our complex helped me because I certainly could use the money. Several of us in the six units where we were living would give a sale from time to time. This was something that I really began to enjoy doing. The complex was on a busy street like my father's home, so we did not have to put signs out. One neighbor particularly liked having the yard sale at the beginning of the month because our rent was due, and the sale gave her a little extra money. I loved our sales and making money that way because it was easy and quick. I get a rush. Plus it's truly like the saying again, "One man's trash is another man's treasure." We didn't hold on, we let go of the things that we no longer needed or wanted. These sales began in Los Angeles, on a street named, La Cienga.

My favorite sale is what I call, "the virgin sale," if they have never had a yard sale before. Sometimes their prices might be very low. They may have something unique that I had not come across before. I love virgin sales because it's possible that I can be the first to set eyes on the merchandise and grab the things that are great for me. Usually the sellers are amazed at finally letting things go and making money at their first yard sale.

Another one of my favorites is kids' lemonade stands and their bake sales. I love the kids. I love to support them no matter what, even if I don't drink or eat it. They light up like I do when they make a sale.

Repeat sales are yard sales by people who give multiple sales throughout the year. That's fine because, of course, they are constantly adding more merchandise. I just prefer the virgin sale. I've never been there, so it's more exciting.

At one of my yard sales, a man bought all the merchandise that I had. He said he was sending it all to Mexico. I got rid of what I didn't want, got paid, and helped someone else. That was so cool. Actually, that happened once again years later when someone bought all I had to sell. It was like having an instant cleanout sale. I call this kind of transaction an "old exchange." Whether bidding at auctions, art galleries, estate sales, car auctions, or even trading baseball cards, this has been going on since people started buying things. It's just one of the many different ways of doing the exchange. In the end, the seller and the buyer can be satisfied.

When I moved from Los Angeles to Rancho Cucamonga, where I lived for nine years, I first lived in an apartment. We were not allowed to have a yard sale because it was known as "semi upscale" and besides, it wasn't popular at that time to have sales at an apartment building. Later, when I really wanted to have a sale, I placed an ad in the paper. I had the sale inside my apartment, and it actually went well. However, I prefer being outdoors. I love the idea of being able to shop or sell in the fresh air instead of being closed in. Plus, there's nothing wrong with airing out all of the merchandise as well.

While living at the apartment I became acquainted with my neighbor. She told me that she liked to go to carport sales. I didn't know what she was referring to, so she explained that it was the same as a yard sale or garage sale. I thought she was talking about swap meets. Later, when she asked me to go with her, initially I had a problem because I liked making money, not spending it. Well, since I couldn't give a sale outside the way I wanted to unless I took my merchandise all the way to my father's house in Los Angeles, I began to drive my neighbor to sales. She taught me how to look for signs on the street and follow them. To this day I'm still getting treasures, and I try very hard not to get junk as I go to sales by "following that sign." In fact, signs are the first step to having a yard sale.

GOOD SIGNS HELP SELLERS SELL
GOOD SIGNS HELP BUYERS BUY

STEP 1: Invest in your signs. The **#1** way of advertising for your yard or garage sale are your signs with the arrows on them. I suggest large neon poster board signs if you live in an area that does not have high traffic flow. Your signage is what's going to make your sale a success or not. You want your buyers to follow that sign and follow that arrow. Make it plain and clear. Try to stick to the same color signs. This makes it easier to get to the property without other distractions. If another sale sign has the same color, just make sure your arrows will lead the people directly to your sale.

A date on your sign is sometimes a good idea because not everyone takes their signs down from the prior week, and then people are just spinning their wheels. Remember to take your signs down after your sale. I know most of the time you just don't feel like it, but we don't want our cities to start fining us. Some cities only allow you to have a couple of sales a year.

Make sure you put your most important eye-catching sign at the main intersection. It's to your advantage to make your signs visible to as much of the ongoing traffic as possible. Lots of traffic is your best friend when having a yard sale. Use that main intersection as a guide to your home.

If the property is not easy for drivers to see, they need specific directions. I have seen many things used as a sign: pieces of cardboard, plain white printer paper, a chair with a teddy bear in it, an easel with a sign on it, people waving their hands, cars with the sign, costumes, balloons, and all sorts of other eye openers. Whatever you decide, make sure that it's going to work for your sale.

Another thing to be mindful of, if you live well into the block away from the busy street, and you notice that no one is coming to your sale, check to make sure your signs are still up. Sometimes, one of your neighbors on the block may have started their sale after you and shoppers are stopping at the neighbor's. You might have to put up another sign right by your neighbor's sale so the people will know to also go to your sale which is further down the block. Neighbors can help each other by communicating and giving the details of their sales so this problem won't happen.

It's almost never necessary to write your address and street name on your yard sale sign because most shoppers don't live near you and they may not know the street anyway. Since everyone does not own a smart phone or GPS yet, the arrows should be sufficient.

Every now and then I have come upon a sale by accident because the signs were pitiful. In that case, I'm sure that it's clear what to do for their next sale: simply have those signs in place for people to follow that sign.

An interesting thing happened while I was working on this book. My neighbor and I were talking as he was getting ready to leave for work on a Monday. He told me that he wanted to give his first yard sale that Saturday, September 24th. He said he would go to all the neighbors to ask if they wanted to participate. My mouth was wide open in disbelief since he had never had one, which gave me such a lift while working on my book. There are approximately 15 houses on our street.

Only about four of us have had sales since I've been on this block. I was so excited! I told him he should put it in the paper. It's a good idea because there isn't a lot of extra traffic coming to this particular street. I was so happy because I wanted to have a sale the prior Saturday, but I didn't want to give it by myself. My least favorite thing about giving a sale is putting up the signs and taking them down, but it' s a must, especially where we are located. We need at least eight signs.

Of course, for some people, putting up the signs might be their most enjoyable thing to do. Some people use their art abilities to make some great signs, you know, "To each his own." The most important thing to remember is that without signs, if you are not already on a busy street, there would be no sale at all. Most of us don't have "invitation only" sales or yard sales just for our neighbors. We want, "Come one, come all."

Well, it turned out that I had the sale in September all alone. No one responded, not even the neighbor who approached me about having the yard sale, but that was OK. I know how to walk alone when I have to, and this is my specialty. When you say the words "yard sale" to me, it turns me on, and I'm ready!

STEP 2: I have found that Saturday is the most popular day to go to a sale and to have one. Sometimes people write Friday, Saturday, and Sunday on their signs for an entire weekend sale, and that's good information because people can choose whether to come back or not. Also, others might join that sale with more merchandise. I know one household that has their sale on a Tuesday, so far once a year. They make it a point to write the word "Tuesday" on their neon sign so that people definitely know it's not a leftover sign from the weekend. That's a very smart move.

In super hot weather, definitely start your sale as early as possible, that way you can make it comfortable for people and you can possibly sell out before noon. So, don't be mad at those early birds. Sometimes, selling cold water for a reasonable price can keep the customers happy in all the heat.

If you pick a windy day to have a sale, make sure your merchandise and signs are secure. You don't want anything to fall on anyone while they are shopping. Also, I have actually seen people take down signs just to be mean, so if they are out of view, it's a good idea from time to time to check to see if they are still up.

When it's cold, consider selling coffee or hot chocolate, or if you have a standing outdoor heating lamp, turn it on. It won't hurt to go that extra mile and make your customers happy. I live in the desert, so it gets very cold in the winter and, of course, super hot in summer, so I am very weather conscious.

Unless your sale is just one particular kind of merchandise such as tools, baskets, lawn furniture, crafts, baby clothes, etc., it's not always necessary to write down your merchandise. Drivers don't have time to read a lot of information on signs. Most shoppers want to come see what you have anyway. They just might find the hidden treasure they are looking for on your table. Another reason to get out early is that a lot of gardeners are out early who just might happen to drive by a yard sale and see a lawn mower or other lawn items before you are ready. So hurry, get out, and go for it.

On a nice warm day, having a yard sale can be as relaxing as a day in the park. If you have help you can even throw some food on the grill outside during your sale, especially if you have a side area.

STEP 3: Check your entire house inside and out. Organize before your sale; go through your things whether they are as small as a hairpin or as big as a house to see what you really want to sell. Check all of the closets, bathrooms, and the kitchen, everywhere with a fine tooth comb. You can unload anything, and you might just enjoy it.

Try to have a neat and clean sale. However, if it's not, people will still buy it and clean it themselves if they want it badly enough.

Go through pockets and purses, sometimes valuables are left inside. I have given back a social security card, personal pictures, and even a little money. Once I bought a little girl's pink bag for my oldest daughter; she was about three years old. When she found two bills in it, she said, "Look, Mommy, two dollars." It was two twenty-dollar bills. I was long gone from that sale and wasn't sure where it was because I had gone to so many others. After that I decided if I'm still on the property and I find money, I will let the people know, and that's all I have to say about that. I have even found $25 in the street while going to a yard sale and no one was there looking for it. Well, in life we all know that sometimes we lose things and sometimes we find things.

STEP 4: Creative yard sale money can be made from other things. I knew someone that needed money, so she started grilling hot dogs outside and made $40. If you are a business person you can set up a table with your business cards on it, you can have samples in baskets of whatever you sell. Yard sales can give you some exposure in your community, so take advantage of it.

On another note, it's a good idea to be watchful of your goods; every now and then things are taken. That's just how it is sometimes. Try to keep jewelry and other small items where you can see them.

Having bags is a good idea for your customers' merchandise. There's no need to buy them. You don't want the extra expense and most customers are fine carrying their items if you don't have bags. Move your vehicles to make space for your customers to park if it's possible.

Individual sale prices will always vary. You may get the person that will pay your price, but remember that nowadays there are a lot of sales and people can just go to the next one as far as prices. However, it's possible to get the price you want.

STEP 5: Prepare as much as you can before the sale. Those Black Friday and day-after-Christmas sales are prepared for the rush. At the same time, I have had spontaneous sales and they went fine. I even assisted someone who planned it the night before. Yard sales can be as easy as 1-2-3: 1. Put your signs out, 2. Open your garage, and 3. Sell the things that you don't want.

STEP 6: Make sure you have change. You don't want to lose any customers, and also you hope the shopper has change as well. You don't want to have to give them $19 change for a dollar item.

STEP 7: Make sure your pets are secure. Once I went to a sale that was in the homeowner's backyard and the lady's turtle was coming full speed ahead towards my leg with its mouth wide open. It scared the heck out of me. I didn't know turtles could move that fast. The lady just laughed and picked it up. Another time when I was at a yard sale, a Great Dane came running out of a neighbor's house; it was so quick that all we could do was stand still.

STEP 8: Music can be a good part of the experience. I suggest that you play music like the stores do. Playing nice music might help your sale, although I wouldn't blast it, you don't want to disturb your neighbors.

STEP 9: Don't forget to be friendly. I once went to a sale where a man and woman were arguing. He scared me and that ran me off, almost like the turtle.

STEP 10: Make sure you have someone to cover for you in case you have to go inside, or especially if you have to go check on your signs. I was in disbelief when a lady left her daughter alone at the sale while she went to put up more signs.

STEP 11: In general, you do want people to start coming as early as possible so you can sell it all and go on with your day. The 6 a.m. early bird might buy your most expensive item. The shoppers who come later may not need that item, so try not to turn anyone away. Sell it all as fast as you can. Most shoppers don't have time to wait for you to open and sell at your leisure because you're not the only one having a sale that day. I'm just saying, starting early gives you the opportunity to get other important things done. I know I try and do as many productive things as possible in one day.

In graduate school my capstone research project was called "How Can a Substitute Teacher Build Community in the Classroom in a Day?" It was about getting in as much teaching as you could by being with the students for a day and utilizing the time spent to accomplish a goal that would have a great impact on the students' futures. I dare to try and get all that I can in a one-day yard sale. Surely sales at any hour can be as successful as early morning sales. It can be a matter of location and your signs in general, so nothing should stop you from trying to have a great sale.

As you already know, everything can be sold at a yard sale like the clothes on your back, even things that you would not think about, like your pet puppies, snakes, and birds. I have seen it. Once there was a big fat black pig on the grass at a house in Rancho Cucamonga, but it wasn't for sale. It was quite an eye catcher. I have the picture to prove it.

The "Big Fat Black PIG"

Step 12: People give sales for many different reasons such as just cleaning out, too much stuff, they want to give someone else a turn, they need money, going through a divorce, want to get rid of memories, death, they're lonely and want to see people, and many more reasons. Some need the money and some don't. It doesn't matter to some people if they get rid of valuables or not, they didn't necessarily need the money, but most people do. At times I have desperately needed money and other times I was able to donate.

DON'T GIVE UP

If you have great signs and get a good amount of customers you should be able to sell your stuff without any problems. If you don't do as well as you would like, don't give up. The person that is looking for what you have, they may come to the next sale, so brighten up those signs.

I think the craziest situation that happened to me at a sale was when I was literally kicked off the property. There was a yard sale that a man had down the block from another sale. He had his things packed together, but he said that everything was free because a charity that he was trying to give it to was too picky, so he decided to give it away to whoever wanted it. Well, I started looking for only what I wanted, and he couldn't believe me, so he asked me to leave just like the charity. I was able to get a few things like the series of *The Godfather* movies, some picture frames, odds and ends. But he seriously asked me to leave, it was shocking and funny. I was embarrassed and I couldn't believe that he was serious, but he was. It was a strange experience, but now I'm glad it happened so I could write about it.

Smart Shopping At Yard Sales

I have truly gotten amazing things for myself and others at yard sales. One of my sisters asked me to look out for some Marilyn Monroe items. Well, it didn't take long; I kept finding things until she told me that was enough. When I was finished getting her the items, I even saw some ornaments of Marilyn Monroe that I should have gotten for their uniqueness. They were simply amazing. However, for some reason I didn't get them.

The other amazing items that the same sister asked me to find for her were some women's handkerchiefs. This was very unique because she wanted antique ones. When I was young I remember seeing my aunt with handkerchiefs. Women would use them to dab perspiration off their faces and maybe wipe away a little makeup, but I don't think they used them too much to blow their noses, maybe just powder them. "OK," I thought, "that was an interesting request," and since I never thought about handkerchiefs I didn't know if they were easy to find or not. It took about a year. One yard sale had a box of colorful scarves. When I took a good look inside, there they were: seven little wrinkled handkerchiefs in a variety of bright colors. Still, the best news yet about these handkerchiefs was the woman selling them was about in her fifties and they were from her grandmother, which definitely made them antiques.

This became very sentimental for me because it was wonderful to be asked to look for them and to actually find them. That was special! The handkerchiefs were $0.25 each and I had them dry cleaned for a dollar each, just because I thought they were delicate and very precious. I gave them to my sister on Thanksgiving Day. She was quite surprised, and it was my pleasure. It goes to show there can be a story behind even finding someone's request. Sometimes we have to diligently search for hidden treasures that mean a lot to us as individuals. Some things are worth the adventure, at least that's what it was to me.

SOMETHING OLD SOMETHING NEW, IT MIGHT BE YOURS AND MINE TOO

I know people that used to be snobs about going to yard sales. They had to have it new. However, when they started seeing that I found some amazing things, they changed and started asking me to look out for their specifics. "Aha!" You never know what you might do later. After all, every time you sleep at a hotel you are sleeping on used bedding. Even the President of the United States has. Every time you go to a restaurant, no matter how fine, those dishes were used by someone else.

There are a lot of people selling brand new items at their yard sales, so if you are a "new only" buyer, it can still be worth the stop!

SOME VALUABLE FINDS

I have had the opportunity to come across many valuables. Some I kept over the years, and some I have lost. I have moved several times to different cities for different reasons. I remember buying a ring when I lived in Rancho Cucamonga, I paid less than $0.50 for it and it was appraised at about $400. Do I have the ring today? No, and it was beautiful. Sometimes when you move, you lose things. I wish I could have held on to more of the treasures that I bought at yard sales. In the mid-nineties I opened a store in Rancho Cucamonga, California, called Barely Worn Children's Resale. I loved my store, and yes, I got my merchandise from yard sales and donations. I had the best barely worn resale store and some unique decorations, such as a life size Fog Horn™ rooster from Warner Brothers™ cartoons, and toddler-sized stuffed dolls of Angelica™, Chuckie™ with his glasses on, and Tommy™ from the *Rugrats*™ cartoon. People always wanted to buy the decorations as much as the merchandise. I only wished that I could have stayed in that city and kept the store, but I moved on.

I also bought an amazing Bible that was from the late 1800s or earlier. It was so delicate that I didn't know how to preserve it. I ended up selling it to an antique store along with some other treasures that I wish I still had. Other things I had were three small pillows from Israel which were handmade. They were adorable. I still have a brown rocking chair in my living room. I'm proud of having it because I know it made all the moving trips.

I know we can't keep it all forever. Even if we made a little museum it would still get passed around from place to place at some point. Even some businesses get passed on. Whether they get passed on or not, some just go out of business. Some stores that were long standing are now gone today.

"*Old Faithful*"

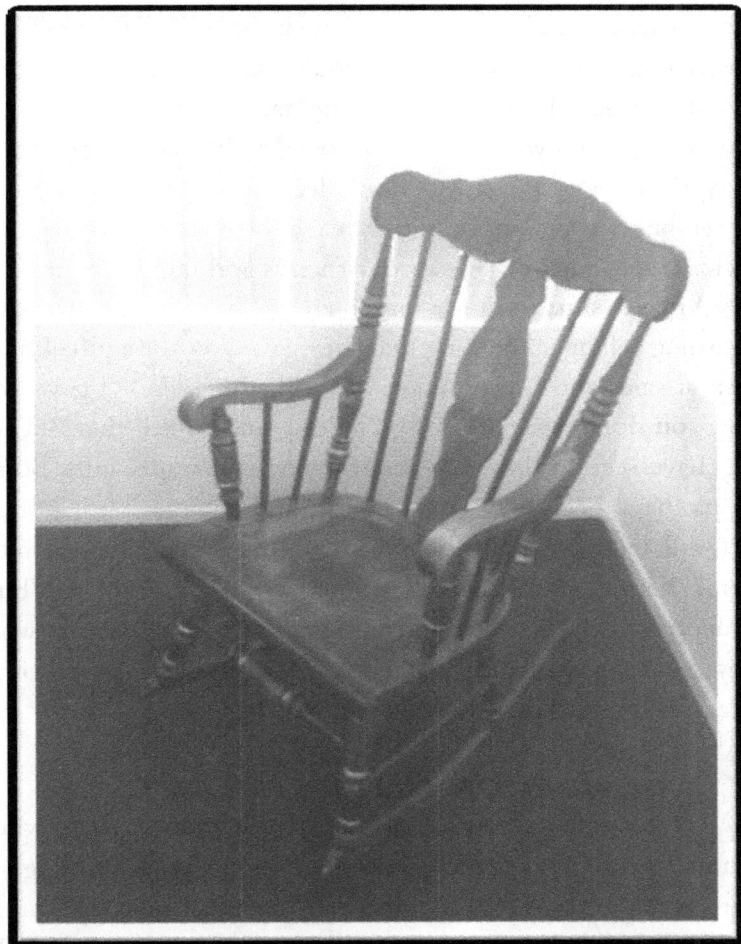

Purchased more than 17 years ago at a yard sale for $40,
retails for more than $250+

GET IT WHILE YOU CAN

A silly thing that I have done in the past when helping some friends and family give their sales is to pass up merchandise that I wanted. I could have been a customer myself, instead I just let someone take what I could have gotten. So, when you have first choice, really take advantage of it. A buyer is a buyer, so don't let it pass you by. I think sometimes we get modest with each other. Also, if you are having a sale and you know your friends and family are coming over, make sure you are prepared to have an explanation regarding selling something that they gave you for a gift. I have been at sales and heard people say something like, "I gave you that, you don't want it?" or "You're going to sell that?" They may have second thoughts about giving you future gifts. Some people have been very embarrassed, and some are just honest and will tell you they don't want it. It's something to think about because most of the time we don't want to hurt someone's feelings. Some kids are good at telling parents what they don't want anymore. Make sure you want to get rid of it. Check on its value (if you want to).

HOLD ON TO IT JUST IN CASE

Have a safe and secure place for your money. Also, when you first get to a sale, take a quick look around at everything. If you are not sure you want something then just hold on to it in case you want it before you leave. If someone comes and picks something up that you had the chance to get first, oh well, too late. That's happened to me many times. All I could do was stare and hope they put it down. Actually, sometimes they did.

Check your merchandise carefully because you never know why people are getting rid of it. Sometimes it may have a flaw that is not too noticeable and they can get away with putting it off on you. Maybe something was glued back together. I know I don't like things that have a crack in them unless it is so sentimental and just the love of my life. For instance, a unique brass vase that I have has a little chipping from the material covering the brass. I still like it very much and I want it to stay visible on my dining table. Sometimes, for something that is really nice and you don't mind paying a good price for it, ask quick questions like, "Why are you getting rid of it?" A little history helps you know it's worth.

I have, of course, brought some things home and realized that they were damaged. Bright sunshine won't always allow you to see spots on white or light clothes. Just take a second to double check before you buy something.

TIME IS OF THE ESSENCE

Time is of the essence when you go to yard sales, so have a quick eye, because yard sales usually only last for the day. People come and go so quickly because they want to catch more and more sales. One sale won't have everything that you want, so you have to keep moving, you know, like you do in the mall.

That's why you get your gas the night before, or get up extra early. It's the same with eating; buy your donuts and coffee or take a snack or two and water. Be prepared ahead of time, try not to stop for bathroom breaks if you can help it, because again, time is of the essence. There are many do's and don'ts about giving and going to yard sales.

First, check the weather for that week, although some people might have a sale no matter if it rains, snows, or hails. In some ads people will let you know if it is an indoor sale because of the weather. Most estate sales are inside, and you usually get to go through the entire house because everything is for sale. So, the weather is no issue in that case, just be weather conscious. Turn off your sprinklers and hope your neighbor's sprinklers won't interfere as well. Keep a large plastic or canvas tarp handy, just in case there is an unexpected downpour.

When going to a yard or garage sale, plan ahead to go early. Walk out your door as soon as daylight hits. Early birds can get there first if an ad was placed in the paper or if the people put their signs up the evening before. The first one there gets first choice. Of course, you can't be at all of them first, but you can try. Who wouldn't want first choice at a one day sale? Anybody who doesn't understand why people get there so early, well, that's why. Either it's first choice or it's gone, just like any other one day sale. Nowadays many people camp out days ahead for the latest phone or game. When I first moved to the Antelope Valley about ten years ago, people were actually camping out to buy homes. I'm a witness because I even did it.

SIGNS ARE IMPORTANT

You will be looking at signs. Hopefully, they will just have arrows to direct you straight to the property. As I said before, bright fluorescent or neon signs are great. They are what I call reflector signs that can capture driver's attention. They are the most visible and the arrows get you right to the point. Remember, people really don't have time to read a lot of writing on the signs, arrows usually work perfectly. As long as we can get to the sales with the signs clearly directing, it can be a smooth sailing experience. Getting from point A to B without too many distractions is wonderful.

OTHER KINDS OF SALES

Community sales are great because you save gas. You walk from one participating home to the next. That is so cool. These are also called block sales or multifamily sales. It's really convenient for people who are going to these sales because the more the merrier. There are more than enough people to buy from all the sellers.

Years ago some churches would have what they called "rummage sales," but you don't hear that phrase as much. The sales now are much nicer than just rummaging through. Sometimes you can go to yard sales before you go to the mall, and you just might find what you are looking for there.

I like it when public and private schools have a big sale on their campus. If you are shopping for kids you can get tons of kids' stuff. I have found that baby clothes and accessories are very easy to find because children grow so fast that they don't even have time to wear things out. Sometimes the things are brand new anyway. It's worth the search.

I find it amusing when I drive up to a property to see who's giving the sale. If I see an elderly couple I know I might see antiques or some things that have been preserved for years and years. If they have some of their parents' things, then there you have it, antiques for sure. It's also interesting when I see a younger couple, because they sometimes have unused wedding gifts, and they may also be getting rid of used but valuable things that their parents gave them to start off with.

I love seeing teen things because at this time I have a teen and she can be very picky. Most of the time you go to yard sales you already know what you are looking for. When I first started going out I didn't have anything in particular that I was looking for, but quickly I found out, whatever you want you will find it.

Again, some people have surprised me with their shopping at yard sales. I know some that seem so perfect. Their home and car and clothing are so immaculate, and low and behold, when they say they got something from a yard sale, well, it's just breathtaking. I shouldn't be so surprised because I do it, but well, I am surprised. Just goes to show yard selling now is big business, and a great big broad marketplace for all to come to.

I even enjoyed watching *America's Next Top Model*™ once when they had the models go to a thrift store to put outfits together to model on the runway. I loved seeing what they put together. It shows that used can work as well as new in just about any event.

You might find the very thing that you are collecting, if you like collecting items. I have seen many people get rid of their collections such as specific animal collections, Beanie Bears™, scrapbooks, and many more interesting things that someone else can enjoy.

One of my many nieces stopped her dolphin collection and sold them at the yard sale, but I have a friend who is holding on to her giraffe collection and has no intention of getting rid of it.

PRICING

I have found some great deals over the years. Again, people's prices certainly can vary; after all, it's your call. There are so many sales nowadays, much more than when I started going in the mid-eighties. So, if one house asks too much you can always go to the next and get a better deal. Some people's prices are exceptionally high, and some are quite low, but whatever the case, it's up to the seller as well as the buyer. Again, sometimes people who have never given a sale may charge a ridiculous amount for something they never used.

It might be OK for some people, but if you are a regular you know that you can move on to the next sale and get it for less.

When I assist friends or family with their yard sales, I prefer that they have their own price in mind. If they leave it entirely up to me, I try to be as fair as possible and I try and get them an extra dollar or two if possible. When going to a sale it never hurts to ask the seller if they are firm on the price. Some people don't mind going down on their prices, so ask and see.

It isn't surprising to see yard sales from the mountain top, to the valley, and to the ocean. People live all over this earth and they give yard sales wherever they are.

In my final summary, I have gone to yard sales in all kinds of neighborhoods. My most beautiful and breathtaking experience was when I was staying at my family's home in Inglewood, California. I drove south on a street named Van Ness to its end, went up into the hills of Palos Verdes, and I went to yard sales. Then I traveled through the hills of Palos Verdes and saw the magnificent view of the ocean. It was most glorious to behold. To top it off, a yard sale was directly across from the beach. It couldn't get better than that. It was too much, and I was very excited. I met a lady at the sale and we discussed how much I loved the ocean view and she suggested that I rent her beach house for a weekend for our family. Unfortunately, I never did. However, one day soon, I will spend a weekend on the beach, see that masterpiece of a view, and possibly have a yard sale.

Jhani Monroe

Jhani's Unique Finds at Yard Sales

Handmade table runner from Israel, a Psalm written in Hebrew. Paid $5 for both, value: $25+

*Jhani purchased a sarong at a yard sale for $0.25.
She gave it to purse designer, Mollie Williams of
Mollie's Handmade One-of-a-Kind Bags, and
Mollie created the Handmade Hobo Drawstring Bag.
Value $45.00*

1492 Santa Maria replica, originally bought as a set with other two ships. Jhani paid $6 for all three. Retail prices range from $18 to $1,800.

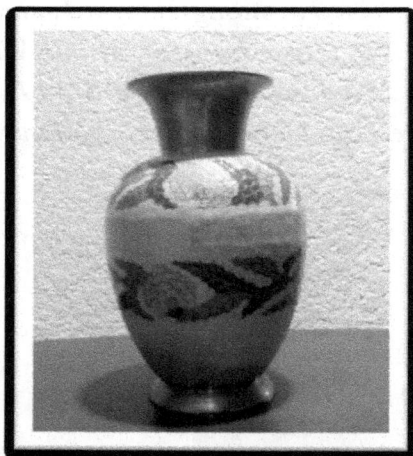

A beautiful brass vase with decorative cover. Paid just a few dollars.

Cheetahs & more cheetahs – in Samara's bedroom. paid $0.10 to a few dollars.

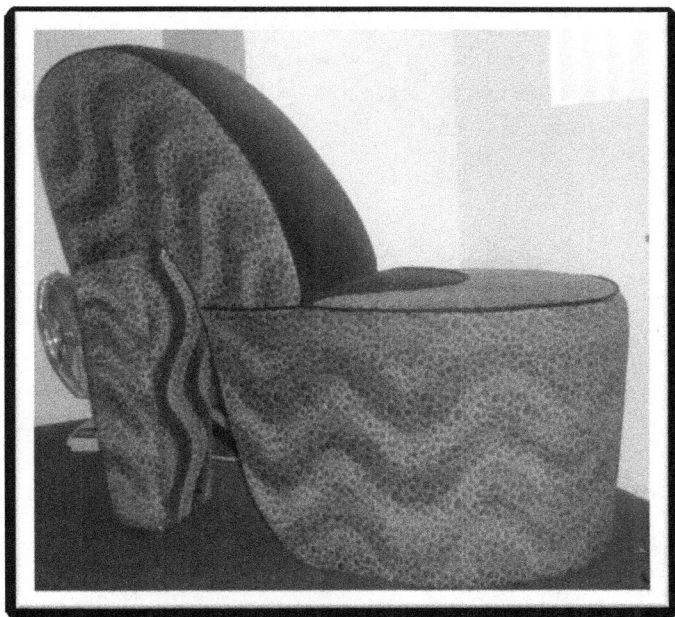

Purchased at yard sale for $20, retails for $200+

ABOUT THE AUTHOR

Johnnie Marie Monroe (Jhani) was born and raised in Los Angeles, California. Her love for yard sales started as a hobby and grew into a business. She has been having yard sales, going to yard sales, and teaching others how to have yard sales for more than 24 years. Encouraged by her youngest son and many others, she decided to take her hobby/business to the next level and write her first book. Jhani holds a Master of Arts degree in Education from Fielding Graduate University in Santa Barbara, California. She has worked in her profession, but when enrollment at the last charter school where she was teaching was too low, the school closed. She was encouraged to work her hobby as a means of making ends meet. Now her passion is her business. Jhani lives in Lancaster, California with her husband, Samuel. They have four children.

A NOTE FROM THE AUTHOR

Yard sales, garage sales, estate sales, and whatever else you want to call them will go on forever, especially in today's economy. They have spread everywhere. I remember when we were building our beautiful home, someone said, "There won't be any yard sales here." Well, less than a couple of weeks after our track was completed and we moved into our homes, the neighbor directly across from me had a moving-in sale. I was shocked and happy. After that I had no problem giving sales every now and then. So, new homes or not, you might just see a yard sale anywhere. Yard sales are a part of our society today and very popular, I might add.

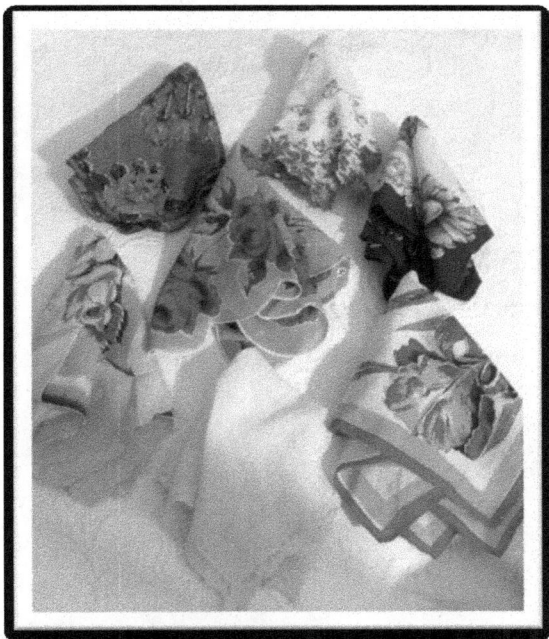

Found these antique handkerchiefs for one of my sisters. Paid $0.25 each, dry cleaned for $1.00 each.

Yard Sale Notes

Yard Sale Notes

www.ingramcontent.com/pod-product-compliance
Lightning Source LLC
Chambersburg PA
CBHW071104040426
42443CB00008B/958